MINNESOTA COOKIN'
by
Bruce Carlson

All rights reserved. No part of this book may be reprodu transmitted in any form or by any means, electronic or cal, except by a reviewer who may quote brief passages review to be printed in a magazine or newspaper.

HEARTS 'N TUMMIES COOKBOOK COMPA
A Dinky Division of Quixote Press

1854 - 345th Avenue, Wever, Iowa 52658
1-800-571-BOOK

© 1994 Bruce Carlson
ISBN: 1-57166-000-3

SO, WHAT'S SO SPECIAL ABOUT MINNESOTA COOKING?

Well, I guess there's nothing particularly special about Minnesota cooking unless you happen to want some of the best dang eatin' in this corner of the universe. Maybe it's something in the clean air blowin' through from the west. Maybe it's all that clear clean water we have in Minnesota. I dunno, but I sure know that some of the world's best cookin' comes right smack out of Minnesota.

Salads	3	Pie	93
Veggies	23	Main Dishes	103
Beverages & Snacks	29	Bread	135
Soup	39	Candy	147
Cookies & Bars	43	Microwave	155
Desserts	69		

SALADS

MINNESOTA SALADS

Apricot Salad....................13
Cherry Salad 6
Chicken Salad 10
Cinnamon Apples 9
Cottage Cheese Salad..........15
Cranberry Salad 5
Cranberry Salad 7
Cucumber Salad..................20
Macaroni Salad 18
Mock Crab Salad.................19

Northwoods Cole Slaw
    Dressing..........................22
Pear Salad 16
Pineapple Star Salad...........11
Quick Jell-O Salad 8
Rhubarb Salad 12
Rigatoni Salad......................17
Salad Dressing 21
Vegetable Salad...................14

CRANBERRY SALAD

1 (3 oz.) pkg. Jello (red flavor; I use raspberry)
1 C. boiling water
¾ C. canned pineapple juice
1 (8 oz.) can whole cranberry sauce
1 C. diced apples
⅓ C. coarsely chopped nuts

Dissolve gelatin in boiling water. Add pineapple juice and cranberries. Chill until slightly thickened. Stir in remaining ingredients. Chill until firm. Recipe may be doubled. Use only 1 C. canned pineapple juice.

CHERRY SALAD

2 pkgs. cherry Jello
2 C. hot water

1 can cherry pie filling

TOPPING:
12 large marshmallows
1 (3 oz.) pkg. cream cheese

1 C. cream

Dissolve Jello in hot water. Stir in pie mix and chill until firm. In a double boiler, melt marshmallows. Fold in cream cheese and whipped cream; spread over set Jello. Note: Rene uses 20 to 30 large marshmallows and 1 pkg. prepared Dream Whip.

CRANBERRY SALAD

1 pkg. cranberries
2 env. plain gelatin
2 C. sugar

1 C. diced pineapple
1 C. white grapes
½ C. walnuts

Cook cranberries in 3 C. of water until tender. Drain through a sieve and get as much of the pulp as possible. Discard the skins. Place on stove and bring to a boil. Add the sugar and the gelatin which has been dissolved in a little water. Remove from stove and cool. When cool add the pineapple, grapes and nuts. Pour into a 9x13-inch dish. A little chopped celery can also be added, if desired.

QUICK JELLO SALAD

8 oz. container cottage cheese

8 oz. mandarin oranges

8 oz. pineapple chunks

8 oz. container Cool Whip

Mix ingredients together. Add small pkg. orange Jello and stir together. Refrigerate for several hours. (Any flavor of Jello may be used.)

CINNAMON APPLES

8-10 Johnathan apples   ½ C. sugar
1 C. red cinnamon candies   8 C. water

Peel and quarter apples. Cook sugar and candies in water until dissolved. Add apples and cook slowly until apples become transparent. (Apples will be soft but do not allow them to fall apart.) Chill. (Amount of sugar and candies will depend on apples sweetness and desired red color.) Use as a salad or on a relish plate.

CHICKEN SALAD

4 C. chopped chicken
1 C. pineapple tidbits (drained)
1 C. chopped walnuts

1 C. seedless grapes
1 C. chopped red apples

Mix above and moisten with mayonnaise. Refrigerate and serve on lettuce leaves.

PINEAPPLE STAR SALAD

1 pkg. lemon Jello
1 large can pineapple (undrained)
2 (3 oz. ea.) pkgs. Phil. cream cheese
1 small can pimento
1/8 tsp. salt

½ C. celery (cut fine)
½ C. walnuts
½ pt. cream (whipped)
   (can use Cool Whip)

Use pineapple juice to make 1 C. (if not enough use water to make 1 C.). Heat juice and mix in dry Jello. When mixture begins to thicken add pineapple and other ingredients. Pour into star mold and chill. *Note: This was my mother's recipe and was especially nice at Christmas time. Any mold is O.K. but is especially pretty in the star mold pan decorated with pimento.

RHUBARB SALAD

4 C. rhubarb
2 C. sugar
1 (3 oz.) pkg. strawberry Jello

2 C. miniature marshmallows
2 C. whipped topping
  (Dream Whip)

Cook rhubarb and sugar over low heat until tender using no water. Stir in Jello and marshmallows. Cool until starts to set. Stir in whipped topping. Refrigerate.

APRICOT SALAD

2 pkgs. orange Jello
2 C. boiling water
1 C. apricot pie filling
1 c. small marshmallows
1 C. orange juice
½ C. sugar
3 T. flour
1 egg
1 C. whipped topping
½ C. grated cheese

Dissolve Jello in boiling water. Add fruit filling and marshmallows. Pour in 9-inch square pan, let set. Combine juice, flour, sugar and egg. Cook until thickened. Let cool, fold in whipped topping. Pour on top of Jello. Sprinkle cheese on top.

VEGETABLE SALAD

1 can French cut green beans
1 can LeSeur peas (drained)
1 can Shoepeg (white) corn
(drained)
1 C. chopped celery
1 onion (diced)

1 green pepper (diced)
1 small jar pimento
¾ C. sugar
1 tsp. salt
½ C. vinegar
½ C. cooking oil

Bring to a boil the sugar, salt and vinegar. Remove from heat and add cooking oil.
Pour over the vegetables and marinate for 18 hours.

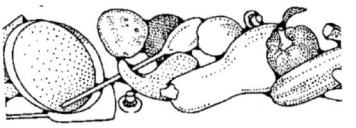

COTTAGE CHEESE SALAD

2 pkgs. lime Jello
1 small can crushed pineapple
1½ C. hot water

1 small container cottage cheese
1 small container Cool Whip

Mix Jello with 1½ C. hot water. When it starts to set, whip with Cool Whip. Add cottage cheese and pineapple.

PEAR SALAD

2 (3 oz. ea.) pkgs. lime Jello
1½ C. boiling water
½ C. cold water

1 (8 oz.) can crushed pineapple
1 (8¼ oz.) can pears
1 C. sour cream

Dissolve Jello in boiling water. Add cold water. Drain fruits and save ⅔ C. syrup.
Add syrup to gelatin mixture. Cool mixture until partially set. Beat in sour cream.
Fold fruits into mixture and pour into 4½ C. ring mold. Chill until set.

RIGATONI SALAD

1 C. onion (chopped fine)
½ C. green pepper (chopped fine)
1 C. Wesson Oil
1 C. celery (chopped)

2 C. sugar
1 C. vinegar
2 tsp. salt
1 tsp. pepper

Cook 12 oz. pkg. rigatoni until done (not soft); drain. Mix sugar, salt, pepper, vinegar and oil. Stir until sugar dissolves. Add remaining ingredients. Pour over macaroni and let stand a few hours before serving.

MACARONI SALAD

1 lb. cooked drained macaroni
3 C. grated carrots
1 small sweet onion (chopped)

1 small pepper
1 pkg. frozen peas (cooked)
Salt and pepper

DRESSING:
2 C. mayonnaise
1 C. sugar

1 C. vinegar
1 can Eagle Brand condensed milk

Mix altogether and refrigerate. This makes a large amount. Would serve at least 12.

MOCK CRAB SALAD

1 C. spaghetti
2 C. chopped celery
1 C. cheese
1 C. pineapple (4 slices)

2 pimentos
1 C. minced onion
½ C. mayonnaise

Break spaghetti into inch pieces and cook until tender in rapidly boiling water, salted. Blanch, drain and chill. Then mix together with all the ingredients. Serve on lettuce with potato chips. Makes 6-8 portions. Very good!

CUCUMBER SALAD

1 (3 oz.) pkg. lime Jello
1 C. boiling water
1 C. cottage cheese

1 C. Miracle Whip
1 medium cucumber
½ medium onion (cut fine)
1 T. vinegar

Pare cucumber; cut out seeds and dice. Dissolve Jello in boiling water. Combine other ingredients, place in blender, add small amount of Jello liquid. Blend. Combine with remainder of Jello. Pour into medium size mold. Chill several hours before serving.

SALAD DRESSING

2 eggs
5 T. apple cider vinegar
1 tsp. dry mustard

2 C. Sunlight or Mazola veg. oil
1 pkg. dry Hidden Valley style dressing

Blend in blender the eggs and vinegar. Add dry mustard. Slowly add oil, then add dry dressing mix. Cover and store in refrigerator.

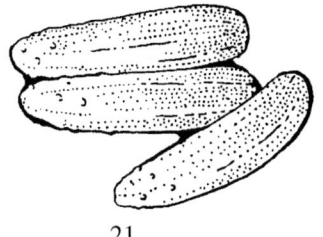

NORTHWOODS COLE SLAW DRESSING

2 C. sugar
1 C. water
1 C. vinegar

1 T. chopped onion
1 tsp. salt
1 tsp. celery seed

Boil sugar and water until it spins a thread. Let cool and then add remaining ingredients. Store in refrigerator.

VEGGIES

MINNESOTA VEGGIES

Broccoli Casserole 27
Broccoli & Rice Casserole 28
Scalloped Cheddar Cheese
   Potato Casserole....................26
Vegetable Casserole 25

VEGETABLE CASSEROLE

2 pkgs. California Blend vegetables (frozen)
1 pkg. shredded cheddar cheese
24 Ritz crackers
1 stick melted butter

Place vegetables (frozen) in casserole; sprinkle cheese on top, then crumble crackers and put on top of cheese (layer) and then drizzle melted butter over all. Bake at 350° for 30 to 45 minutes till brown on top.

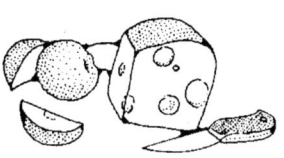

SCALLOPED CHEDDAR CHEESE POTATO CASSEROLE

32 oz. frozen hash browns
½ stick melted butter
¼ tsp. salt
1 can cream of chicken soup
1 pt. sour cream

½ tsp. pepper
½ medium onion (diced)
10 oz. pkg. grated cheddar cheese
Corn flake crumbs

Grease 9x13-inch pan. Mix all ingredients together (except corn flake crumbs) and pour into pan. Melt ¼ C. oleo and 2 C. cornflake crumbs; sprinkle over top and bake at 350° for 1 to 1 ½ hours. (Note: Bonnie ues 1 tsp. salt, 2 T. minced onion, 2 C. grated cheese and mixes crumbs and ¼ C. oleo for topping.)

BROCCOLI CASSEROLE

Put in casserole:
2 pkgs. chopped broccoli (cooked)　　　½ small onion (sauteed in butter)
1 C. cooked rice

ADD:
1 can cream of mushroom soup　　　　　½ C. Velveeta cheese

Top with bread crumbs. Bake 30 minutes.

BROCCOLI AND RICE CASSEROLE

1 pkg. frozen chopped broccoli
½ C. chopped onion (optional)
½ C. chopped celery (optional)
1 can cream of chicken soup

1 C. water
¾ C. canned milk
1 small jar Cheese Whiz
1 C. minute rice

Cook until done according to directions on box - broccoli, onion and celery. When broccoli is done, drain and add 1 T. oleo. Cook soup, water, canned milk, Cheese Whiz and rice. Stir this mixture often as the cheese will cause it to burn. Combine with first ingredients. Pour into baking dish and bake in a 350° oven for 30 minutes. This can be prepared a day ahead and refrigerated until ready to use.

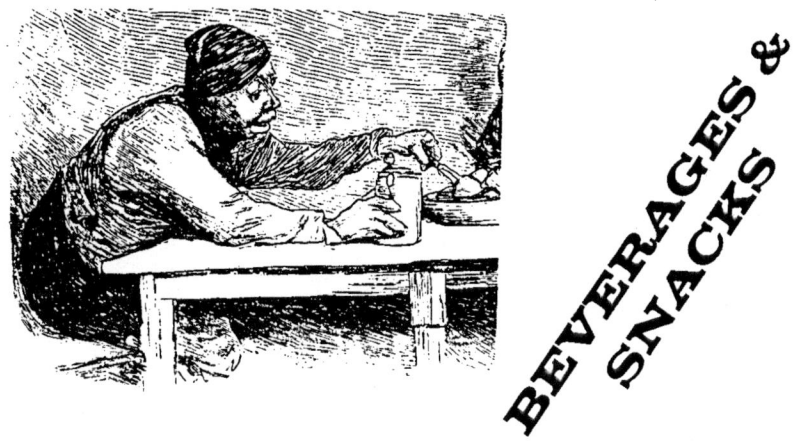

BEVERAGES & SNACKS

MINNESOTA BEVERAGES & SNACKS

Frozen Fruit Slush 31
Garden Pizza 33
Parmesan Cheese Puffs 35
Party Cheese Ball 34
Party Dip for Crackers 36
Rose Wassail 37
Yuletide Punch 32

FROZEN FRUIT SLUSH

- 2 C. water
- 1 C. sugar
- 6 bananas (diced)
- 1 (#2) can crushed pineapple (undrained)
- 1 (12 oz.) can orange juice (mix with ½ C. water)
- 1 jar maraschino cherries (cut in half) (use half of the juice)

Boil together the water and sugar. Mix fruit and juice altogether and then add to syrup; freeze.

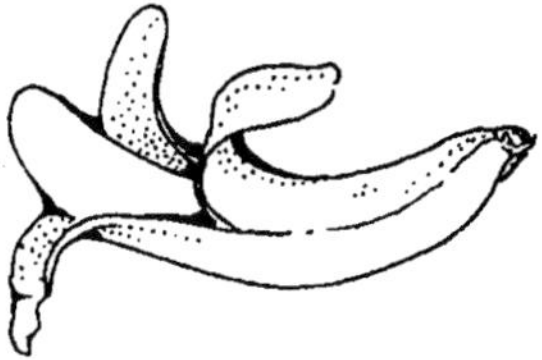

YULETIDE PUNCH

2 pts. raspberry sherbet
1 C. lemon juice
1 (32 oz.) bottle cranberry juice
  cocktail (chilled)

1 C. orange juice
¾ C. sugar
2 (28 oz. ea.) bottles ginger ale
  (chilled)

Let 1 pint sherbet soften. In punch bowl combine it with citrus juices and sugar; stir to dissolve sugar, add ginger ale and cranberry juice. With ice cream scoop float remaining 1 pint sherbet on top of punch. Makes about 20 (6 oz. ea.) servings.

GARDEN PIZZA

2 pkgs. crescent dinner rolls
8 oz. pkg. cream cheese
½ C. Miracle Whip
1 tsp. onion flakes
½ tsp. garlic salt
½ tsp. salt
1 C. chopped green pepper
1 C. chopped tomatoes
1 C. chopped carrots
½ C. chopped onion
Chopped stuffed or ripe olives (optional)

FIRST LAYER: Lay out dinner rolls flat in jelly roll pan. Bake according to directions and cool.

SECOND LAYER: Mix together the cream cheese, Miracle Whip, onion flakes, garlic salt and salt. Spread on cooled crust.

THIRD LAYER: Sprinkle with green pepper, tomatoes, carrots, onion or any combination of fresh vegetables. Refrigerate for several hours.

PARTY CHEESE BALL

8 oz. pkg. cream cheese (softened)   ½ C. grated onion
4 oz. blue cheese (crumbled)   1 T. Worcestershire sauce
8 oz. sharp cheddar cheese (shredded)

Combine cheeses in mixing bowl. Cream until light and well blended. Add grated onion and Worcestershire sauce; mix well. Chill cheeses. Shape cheese into ball and decorate by rolling in crushed pecans or chopped parsley.

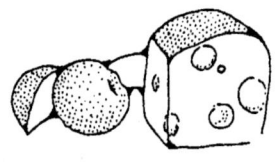

PARMESAN CHEESE PUFFS

1 C. water	⅓ C. butter
1 tsp. salt	1/8 tsp. pepper
1 C. flour	5 eggs (divided)
1 C. grated Parmesan cheese	8 oz. sharp cheddar cheese (cubed)

Bring water, butter, salt and pepper to boil. Remove from heat and stir in flour all at once. Return to low heat and stir mixture until it forms a ball and leaves sides of pan. Cool slightly. Beat in 4 eggs, one at a time, beating well after each. Stir in Parmesan cheese and blend well. Drop by rounded teaspoonfuls onto greased cookie sheet. Beat remaining egg with fork, brush top of puffs only. Bake at 425° until puffed and golden, about 15 to 20 minutes. Remove from cookie sheet and with point of sharp knife, make small slash in side of each puff to let out steam. Cool completely. When ready to serve, cut off tops of puffs, place cube of cheddar cheese in each puff. Reheat at 375° for about 8 minutes or until cheese is melted. Serve warm.

PARTY DIP FOR CRACKERS

1 can tomato soup
1 small pkg. cream cheese
1 small pkg. lemon Jello

½ C. onion (chopped fine)
½ C. celery (chopped fine)
½ C. green pepper (chopped fine)

Mix the first 3 ingredients together and heat until cheese is melted and thoroughly mixed. Cool, then add remaining ingredients. Add any other seasonings, to taste.

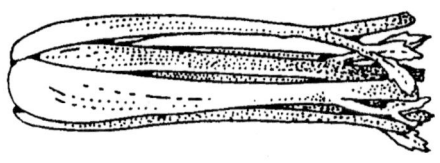

ROSE WASSAIL - (Christmas Punch)

1 pt. cranberry juice cocktail juice
1 (6 oz.) can frozen orange juice concentrate (thawed)
2 C. water
1 T. sugar
¼ tsp. allspice
1 bottle (3¼ C.) dry sauterne

In large kettle combine first 5 items. Bring "almost" to simmering, add last item and heat thru, don't boil. Optional: Add a few drops red food coloring. Stud thick orange slices with whole cloves. Pour into preheated punch bowl and float orange slices atop. Makes 12-14 servings. (Toast with greeting "was haile". Anglo Saxon greeting meaning "YOUR HEALTH!")

38

SOUP

MINNESOTA SOUP

Clam Chowder 42
Garbonzo Bean Soup 41

GARBONZO BEAN SOUP

3 cans garbonzo beans
4-6 diced potatoes
2 green peppers (chopped)
1 large onion (Bermuda) (chopped)
1 lb. bacon (cut-up)
½ lb. diced ham

1 T. oregano
1 T. basil
2-4 bay leaves
2-3 tomatoes (chopped) or
   1 (16 oz.) can tomatoes
Red pepper, salt & pepper, to taste

Simmer all ingredients at least 4 hours. (Works great in crock pot.)

CLAM CHOWDER

2 cans clams	¾ C. flour
1 C. chopped onion	1 pint Half and Half
1 C. chopped celery	1½ tsp. salt
2 C. diced potatoes	Dash pepper
½ C. margarine	1 qt. milk

Drain juice from clams and add juice to vegetables. Cover with water and boil. Melt butter, add flour, stir about 2 minutes. Add milk and Half and Half. Cook, stir with wire whip until smooth and bubbly. Add vegetable mixture with about half of water (sometimes all the water if mixture is quite thick). Add clams. Heat for serving.

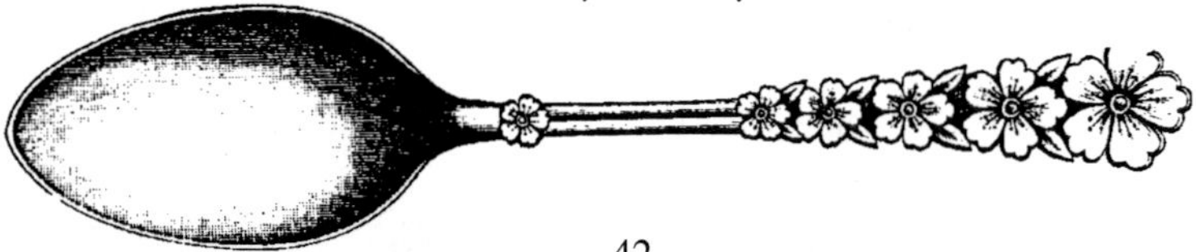

COOKIES & BARS

MINNESOTA COOKIES & BARS

Banana Bars........................67
Best Brownies....................57
Brownies 63
Brown Sugar Cookies...........50
Cherry Bars 58
Chocolate Delights 49
Christmas
    Sugar Cookies.................48
Date Cookies (no bake).........65
Ginger Creams.....................66
Gingersnaps 46
Isanti Cookies 53
Lem-O-Nut Bars 56

Logger's Cookies 54
Mom's Cookie Recipe 61
Peanut Butter Bars..............45
Pine Island Sugar Cookies....51
Pumpkin Bars......................60
Raisin Cookies 55
Salted Nut Bars 59
Sugar Cookies......................62
Stir-N-Drop Sugar Cookies ..52
Syrup Brownies 47
Toffee Butter Bars................68
Zucchini Bars 64

PEANUT BUTTER BARS

1½ C. graham cracker crumbs
½ lb. butter

1 C. peanut butter
1 lb. powdered sugar

Melt the butter and mix with all other ingredients. Pat into a 9x13-inch pan and put in refrigerator to chill. Melt 2 C. of chocolate chips and spread on top.

GINGERSNAPS

2 C. flour
1 T. ginger
2 tsp. soda
1 tsp. cinnamon
½ tsp. salt

¾ C. shortening
1 C. sugar
1 egg
¼ C. molasses
Granulated sugar (optional)

Mix and sift the first 5 ingredients. Sift again twice, return to sifter. Beat shortening until creamy. Add 1 C. sugar gradually. Continue to beat and beat in egg and molasses. Sift a fourth of the flour mixture over molasses mixture. Stir to blend well. Repeat until all flour mixture is added. Form teaspoons of dough in small balls. Roll in sugar and place 2-inches apart on ungreased sheets. Bake at 350° for 12 minutes or until tops are slightly rounded and crackly. Cool on racks. Makes 48 cookies.

SYRUP BROWNIES

½ C. margarine (1 stick)
1 C. sugar
4 eggs (slightly beaten)
1 lb. can Hershey syrup

1 C. + 1 heaping T. flour
½ tsp. baking powder
Nuts

Pour into 10½x16-inch cookie sheet. Bake at 350° for 20 to 25 minutes. Frost with chocolate frosting.

CHRISTMAS SUGAR COOKIES

1½ C. shortening
1½ C. brown sugar
1 egg
1 T. orange juice
½ T. lemon juice

1 C. ground blanched almonds
½ tsp. cinnamon
3 C. flour
½ tsp. salt

Mix shortening, sugar and egg; cream well. Add juices; beat until light and foamy. Add dry ingredients which have been sifted together; add nuts. Chill for at least 3 hours. Roll very thin and cut in fancy shapes. Bake at 375° for 10 minutes - burns easily. Dip immediately in white sugar. Keeps well.

CHOCOLATE DELIGHTS

1 (12 oz.) pkg. chocolate chips
¼ C. butter or margarine
1 C. flour
1 tsp. vanilla
1 (14 oz.) can sweetened condensed milk
1 tsp. milk
1 C. chopped nuts (optional)

Melt chips and butter in saucepan over low heat. Stir in remaining ingredients and mix thoroughly. Drop from teaspoon on greased cookie sheet. Bake at 350° for 6 to 8 minutes. Should appear moist and under-done. Makes 4 dozen cookies.

BROWN SUGAR COOKIES

1½ C. brown sugar
1 C. butter or shortening
2 eggs
½ C. sour milk
1 tsp. soda in hot water

1 tsp. nutmeg
½ tsp. salt
1 C. raisins and nuts
3 C. flour

Mix all ingredients and bake.

PINE ISLAND SUGAR COOKIES

1½ C. powdered sugar
2 sticks oleo or butter (softened)
2½ C. flour (sifted)
1 tsp. baking soda
1 tsp. cream of tartar
1 tsp. vanilla
½ tsp. almond flavoring
2 eggs (beaten)

Cream powdered sugar and oleo; add eggs. Add vanilla and almond extract. Sift flour, soda and cream of tartar. Add to mixture. Bake cookies at 350° till lightly browned around edges. Cookies may be dropped by the spoonful for big, fluffy cookies. Or the dough may be chilled so they can be rolled and cut with cookie cutters, pressed from a ball with a fork or pressed flat with a glass, dipped in sugar before baking.

STIR-N-DROP SUGAR COOKIES

⅔ C. oil
2 tsp. vanilla
¾ C. sugar
2 eggs

2 C. sifted flour
2 tsp. baking powder
½ tsp. salt

Blend oil, vanilla and sugar; add eggs and beat until thickens. Sift together and
stir in creamed mixture the flour, baking powder and salt. Drop by teaspoonfuls
2-inches apart on ungreased cookie sheet. Flatten with greased bottom of glass,
dipped in sugar. Bake until delicate brown. Remove from cookie sheet immediately.
Bake at 375° for 8 to 10 minutes. Makes 3 dozen 3-inch cookies.

ISANTI COOKIES

- 1 C. white sugar
- 1 C. brown sugar
- 1 C. oleo
- 1 C. corn oil
- 1 egg
- 1 C. Rice Krispies
- 1 C. shredded coconut
- 1 C. quick oatmeal
- ½ C. nuts
- 1 tsp. vanilla
- 1 tsp. salt
- 1 tsp. soda
- 1 tsp. cream of tartar
- 3½ C. flour

Mix all together. Roll into balls and flatten with fork. Bake at 350° for 10 minutes. Makes approximately 60 cookies. (Hint: Add Rice Krispies by hand so that mixer does not crush them.)

LOGGER'S COOKIES

2 sticks margarine
4 T. sugar
2 C. flour

1 tsp. vanilla
¼ tsp. peppermint extract
Few drops green food coloring

Make a dough by mixing together margarine, sugar (4 T. is correct), flour and flavorings. Form small balls by rolling pieces of dough between your palms. Place on ungreased cookie sheet and press gently with fingers. Bake at 325° for about 20 minutes. Cool for a minute or so, then place a small Hershey square or chocolate star in center of each cookie. Spread into a circle and place a pecan half in center. Makes about 45 cookies.

RAISIN COOKIES

1½ C. raisins
1 C. water
1 C. shortening (part butter)
1½ C. sugar
½ tsp. salt

3 eggs
3½ C. flour
1 tsp. soda
1 tsp. vanilla

Boil raisins and water until dry. Cream shortening and sugar. Add eggs and mix well. Add flour, soda and vanilla. Fold in raisins. Cool in refrigerator. Roll in balls and dip top in sugar. Bake at 350° for 5 minutes on bottom rack, then move to top rack until light brown.

LEM-O-NUT BARS

2 C. flour
½ C. butter
¼ C. brown sugar
3 eggs (well-beaten)
2 C. brown sugar
½ tsp. salt

1 C. finely shredded coconut
½ C. seedless raisins
½ C. walnuts (chopped)
2 T. lemon juice
1 tsp. grated lemon rind

Mix together thoroughly the flour, butter and brown sugar. Press firmly into greased 9x13-inch pan. Bake at 350° for 10 minutes. Mix eggs, 2 C. brown sugar and salt. Stir in coconut, raisins, walnuts, lemon juice and lemon rind. Spread over partially baked bottom layer. Bake at 350° for 25 minutes. Top will be lightly browned. Cut when cool. Makes 28 bars.

BEST BROWNIES

2 sq. chocolate or ⅓ C. cocoa	1 tsp. baking powder
¼ C. butter	1 tsp. vanilla
1 C. sugar	1 C. nuts (chopped)
½ C. flour	2 unbeaten eggs

Mix together and pour into greased 8x8-inch pan. Bake at 350° for 30 minutes.

FROSTING:

1 stick oleo	1 lb. powdered sugar
4 T. cocoa	1 tsp. vanilla
4-6 T. milk	1 C. chopped nuts

Boil together oleo, cocoa and milk. Add powdered sugar, vanilla and nuts. Ice cake while hot right from the oven.

CHERRY BARS

1 C. oleo	3 C. flour
1 ¾ C. sugar	1 ½ tsp. baking powder
4 eggs	½ tsp. salt
1 tsp. vanilla	1 can cherry pie filling

Cream oleo and sugar together. Add eggs and vanilla. Mix in flour, baking powder and salt. Pour ¾ dough into a greased cookie sheet. Spread cherry filling on top of dough. Drop the remaining dough by tablespoon on top of filling. Bake at 350° for 20 to 25 minutes. Note: When cool, a powdered sugar frosting may be drizzled over bars.

SALTED NUT BARS

FIRST LAYER:
3 C. flour (sifted)
1½ C. brown sugar (packed)
1 C. butter or margarine (softened)
1 tsp. salt

SECOND LAYER:
½ C. light corn syrup
2 T. butter or margarine
1 T. water
1 C. butterscotch chips
2 C. deluxe mixed nuts

Combine flour, brown sugar, butter and salt; blend well. Press into ungreased 15½x10½x1-inch jelly roll pan. Bake at 350° for 10 to 12 minutes. In small saucepan, combine corn syrup, butter, water and chips. Boil for 2 minutes, stirring constantly. Sprinkle nuts over partially baked crust. Pour cooked mixture over nuts. (Make sure all nuts are covered.) Return to oven and bake an additional 10 to 12 minutes or until golden brown. Cool and cut into bars. Yield: 48 bars.

PUMPKIN BARS

2 C. pumpkin (1 can)	2 tsp. baking powder
1 C. salad oil	4 eggs
2 C. sugar	1 tsp. vanilla
2 C. flour	1 tsp. soda
1 tsp. cinnamon	½ tsp. salt

Mix all together until well blended. Grease and flour large cookie sheet with sides. Bake at 350° for 20 to 25 minutes.

CREAM CHEESE FROSTING:

3 oz. cream cheese	1 T. milk
2½ C. sifted powdered sugar	1 tsp. vanilla
	(may substitute lemon extract)

Mix well, adding milk a little at a time.

MOM'S COOKIE RECIPE

½ C. brown sugar
½ C. margarine
1 small box instant pudding
  (any flavor you wish)

1 egg
1¼ C. flour
1 tsp. cream of tartar
1 tsp. soda

Mix all together. Roll in balls and place on cookie sheet. Makes about 30 cookies Bake at 375° for 10-12 minutes.

SUGAR COOKIES

1 C. granulated sugar	2 tsp. vanilla
1 C. powdered sugar	1 tsp. cream of tartar
1 C. margarine	1 tsp. soda
1 C. oil	5¼ C. flour
2 eggs (well beaten)	Granulated sugar or sprinkles

Cream sugars with margarine; add beaten eggs. Stir in oil and vanilla. Mix dry ingredients and blend in. Refrigerate overnight. Form into balls, dip in granulated sugar or sprinkles, and flatten with bottom of glass. Bake at 350° until lightly browned.

BROWNIES

1 large can Hershey's chocolate syrup	4 eggs
1 C. + 1 T. flour	1 tsp. vanilla
1 C. sugar	½ C. nuts (chopped)
1 stick oleo	½ tsp. baking powder

Cream together sugar and oleo. Add eggs one at a time and beat well. Add chocolate syrup. Then add flour and baking powder that have been sifted together, add nuts and vanilla. Bake on large cookie sheet, 10x15-inch, that has been well greased and floured. Bake 30 minutes or until done to touch.

FROSTING:

6 T. oleo	1½ C. white sugar
6 T. milk	½ C. chocolate chips

Mix together, boil ½ minute, remove from heat. Add chips, stir until melted. Spread on brownies.

ZUCCHINI BARS

4 eggs	1 tsp. soda
1 C. salad oil	1 tsp. baking powder
2 C. sugar	½ tsp. salt
1 C. zucchini (raw, peeled)	2 tsp. cinnamon
1 C. nutmeats	2 C. flour

Beat oil and eggs, add sugar and mix throughly. Then add the rest of the ingredients and mix well. Add nuts last. Pour in 11x15-inch cookie sheet which has been greased. Bake 20 minutes in a 350° oven.

FROSTING:

3 oz. cream cheese	¾ lb. powdered sugar
6 T. oleo	1 tsp. vanilla

Mix and frost bars when cool.

DATE COOKIES (NO BAKE)

1 stick oleo
1 C. dates (chopped fine)
1 C. sugar
1 beaten egg

3 C. Rice Krispies
1 C. nuts (chopped)
1 tsp. vanilla
Grated coconut

Melt oleo, add dates, sugar and beaten egg. Cook over medium heat, stirring constantly, until mixture is thick and brown. Remove from heat and add vanilla and nuts. Pour mixture over the Rice Krispies and mix well. Let cool, make into balls or logs and roll in grated coconut.

GINGER CREAMS

½ C. shortening
1 C. sugar
1 egg
1 C. molasses

4 C. flour
½ T. salt
2 tsp. soda
4 tsp. pumpkin pie spice
1 C. hot water

Cream shortening, sugar, egg, molasses until creamy. Add ½ flour, salt, spices, hot water. Beat until smooth. Add remaining flour, drop by spoonsfull. Bake at 350° for 15-25 minutes until done. Frost with powdered sugar.

BANANA BARS

1½ C. flour	½ tsp. soda
1 C. sugar	½ tsp. salt
½ C. margarine	1 tsp. lemon juice
2 eggs	1-2 ripe bananas (mashed)
⅓ C. milk	

Combine and beat 2 minutes. Pour into 9x13-inch greased pan.

TOPPING:

⅔ C. sugar	¼ C. margarine
⅓ C. flour	¼ tsp. nutmeg

Combine and crumble over top. Bake at 350° for 30-35 minutes.

TOFFEE BUTTER BARS

1 C. butter or oleo
1 C. brown sugar
1 egg
1 tsp. vanilla

1 (6 oz.) pkg. chocolate chips
¼ C. chunky peanut butter
¾ C. chopped walnuts
2 C. flour

Cream together butter and brown sugar. Add egg, vanilla and flour. Press into 9x13-inch pan. Bake 15-20 minutes. Melt chips with peanut butter. Spread over bars. Sprinkle with walnuts.

DESSERTS

MINNESOTA DESSERTS

Apple Spice Cake 87
Banana Split Dessert 82
Bread Pud./Van.Sauce....73
Cherry Cheesecake 84
Chilled Strawbry Cream..72
Chocolate Sundae...........80
Cold Water Cocoa
  Cake.............................90
Company Time Cake 85
Cream Puff Dessert.........75
Danish Cream 71
Freeborn Frosting...........86
Fruit Soup 78

Great Lakes Apple
  Dumplings....................77
Homemade Vanilla
  Ice Cream 76
Lemonade Dessert 74
Luscious Lutheran
  Cake.............................92
Old Fash.Peach Cake 88
Oreo Cookie Dessert 81
Pistachio Ice Cream 83
Raspberry Dessert 79
Rhubarb Crunch.............89
Rhubarb Cobbler 91

DANISH CREAM

4 C. Half & Half
4 C. sugar
1½ T. + ½ tsp. unflavored gelatin

4 C. sour cream
2 tsp. vanilla

Combine sugar and gelatin. Stir into Half and Half. Heat slowly until sugar and gelatin are dissolved. Remove from heat and cool until slightly thickened. Stir in sour cream and vanilla. Portion into dishes. Chill and top with thickened raspberries. Makes about 25 servings (5 oz. each).

CHILLED STRAWBERRY CREAM

2 C. vanilla wafers
½ C. soft butter
1 C. powdered sugar
1 tsp. vanilla

1/8 tsp. salt
2 eggs
1 qt. (about) strawberries (sliced)
1 C. whipping cream

Line glass baking dish with half of crumbs. Cream butter with electric mixer and gradually add sugar. Add vanilla, salt, and beat until fluffy. Add eggs, one at a time, beating well after each addition. Spread mixture carefully over crumbs in dish. Arrange sliced berries in layer over creamed mixture. Whip cream and spread over berries. Sprinkle crumbs over whipped cream and refrigerate at least 3 hours.

BREAD PUDDING WITH VANILLA SAUCE

6 eggs
1½ C. sugar
¼ tsp. salt
½ tsp. vanilla

3 C. milk
1 C. Carnation milk
3-4 slices raisin bread (cubed)

Mix ingredients together and pour over cubed raisin bread in 9x13-inch pan. Bake at 300° for 45 minutes.

VANILLA SAUCE:
1 C. sugar
1½ T. cornstarch
2 C. hot water

1 T. vanilla
3 T. butter

Mix sugar and cornstarch together. Add hot water, cook until clear and thick. Remove from heat and add vanilla and butter; blend. Serve hot with bread pudding.

LEMONADE DESSERT

2 pkgs. Toll House crackers
¼ C. powdered sugar
1 stick margarine (melted)

1 can sweetened condensed milk
1 (6 oz.) can frozen lemonade
1 medium size container Cool Whip

Crush crackers. Mix with powdered sugar and melted margarine. Press into 9x13-inch pan and refrigerate while making topping. Save some crumbs for top of dessert. Mix milk, lemonade and Cool Whip. Spread over top of crust. Sprinkle a few crumbs on this. Keep in refrigerator.

CREAM PUFF DESSERT

1 C. water
1 stick oleo
1 C. flour
4 eggs
1 large pkg. vanilla instant pudding

3 C. milk
1 (8 oz.) pkg. cream cheese
Cool Whip
Chocolate syrup

Mix water and oleo. Bring to a boil and add flour. Cool and add eggs, 1 at a time. Spread into 9x13-inch pan. Bake at 400° for 30 minutes. Beat all together the pudding, milk and cream cheese. Spread over crust and top with Cool Whip. Sprinkle chocolate syrup over this.

HOMEMADE VANILLA ICE CREAM

4-5 eggs
1½ C. sugar
1 T. vanilla

½ qt. cream or
  2 cans Carnation milk
1 qt. milk

Beat eggs until thick, then add sugar. Beat until thick and light. Add vanilla and cream. Place in freezer and add milk. Freeze with electric ice cream freezer or hand crank freezer.

GREAT LAKES APPLE DUMPLINGS

2 C. flour
½ tsp. salt
⅓ C. shortening

1½ tsp. baking powder
⅔ C. milk
6-8 apples

Mix all ingredients except apples together and roll dough out on lightly floured surface. Cut into 6-8 square pieces. Put one apple, peeled and sliced, on each dough square. Sprinkle over each apple about 1 T. sugar and some cinnamon. Wrap dough around apple and place in 9x13-inch baking dish. Melt 1 C. sugar in 2 C. boiling water and ½ C. butter or margarine. Pour mixture over dumplings and bake until apples are done and top is brown. Bake at 400° for 35-40 minutes.

FRUIT SOUP

3 T. minute tapioca
1 C. cold water
Dash salt
½ C. sugar
Let stand 5 minutes

1 can fruit cocktail (juice and all)
1 can chunk or crushed pineapple
2-3 sliced bananas
1 can mandarin oranges
   (if desired)

Cook 6-8 minutes the tapioca and water and sugar until clear, stirring often. Remove from heat, when cool add the fruits. For diabetics instead of sugar use 5 packets Equal or Sweet and Low, adding this after the tapioca is cooled. For fruit for diabetics, use unsweetened pineapple, fruit cocktail, bananas; and mandarin oranges can be used by using the juice and rinsing the oranges in cool water.

RASPBERRY DESSERT

1 stick oleo + 1 T.
2 T. sugar
1 C. flour

Mix together well. Press in a greased 9x13-inch pan and bake at 325° for 15 minutes. Cool.

MIX TOGETHER WELL:
2 (8 oz. ea.) pkgs. cream cheese (room temperature)
2 C. powdered sugar

Fold in 2 C. Cool Whip or 1 pkg. Dream Whip (prepared). Pour on cooled crust and refrigerate. In a separate bowl dissolve 2 (3 oz. ea.) boxes raspberry Jello and 2 C. boiling water. When dissolved, add 2 pkgs. (about 2 C.) frozen red raspberries. These need not be thawed as added to hot Jello. Pour on top of cream cheese layer and refrigerate until firm.

CHOCOLATE SUNDAE

1 pkg. graham crackers
  (make into crumbs)
1 (6 oz.) pkg. chocolate chips
2 C. powdered sugar

½ gallon soft ice cream
¼ lb. margarine
3 eggs
¾ C. pecans (optional)

Line bottom of 9x13-inch pan with crumbs reserving a little for top. Melt chips and margarine. Stir in eggs, sugar, nuts. Pour over crumbs. Let this harden somewhat before adding ice cream and crumbs. Freeze.

OREO COOKIE DESSERT

- 1 (20 oz.) pkg. Oreo sandwich cookies
- ½ C. (1 stick) oleo (melted)
- 1 (8 oz.) pkg. cream cheese
- 1 C. powdered sugar
- 2 (8 oz. ea.) containers Cool Whip or 1 (16 oz.) container
- 1 large pkg. instant chocolate pudding
- 1 small pkg. instant chocolate pudding

Crush package of Oreo cookies and spread in 9x13-inch pan, holding ½-⅔ C. to sprinkle on top. Pour melted oleo over cookie crumbs. Bake 5-7 minutes at 350°. Cool. While cooling, cream together softened cream cheese and powdered sugar, then add 8 oz. Cool Whip and mix. Spread this over Oreo crust. Make instant puddings - less ½ C. milk - and spread on top of the cream mixture. Then add the other 8 oz. Cool Whip. Sprinkle remaining cookie crumbs over top. Refrigerate, chilling thoroughly before eating. Cut in squares and serve.

BANANA SPLIT DESSERT

½ C. butter (melted)
1 C. flour
½ C. chopped nuts
2 eggs
1 C. butter
2 C. powdered sugar

3-4 bananas, sliced & dipped in juice
1 (20 oz.) can crushed pineapple
 (drained)
2 (10 oz. ea.) pkgs. frozen
 strawberries or 2 C. fresh
Cool Whip
Chopped nuts

Mix melted butter, flour and nuts together; spread in 9x13-inch pan. Bake at 375° for 10 minutes; cool. Mix together eggs, butter and powdered sugar. Beat for 15 minutes. Spread on top of crust. Add the fruit in the following order (in layers): Bananas, pineapple and strawberries. Top with Cool Whip and sprinkle with chopped nuts; chill.

PISTACHIO ICE CREAM DESSERT

18 single graham crackers (2½ x 2½)
12 soda crackers
1 stick margarine

Crush crackers and mix margarine. Put in bottom of 9x13-inch pan.

BEAT AND MIX:
2 pkgs. instant pistachio pudding
2 C. milk
1 qt. softened vanilla ice cream

Pour mixture over cracker crust. Top with 1 pkg. Dream Whip and crush 2 Heath candy bars and sprinkle on top; refrigerate.

CHERRY CHEESECAKE

2 (8 oz. ea. pkgs.) cream cheese (softened)
¾ C. sugar
2 eggs

1 tsp. vanilla
24 vanilla wafers
21 oz. can cherry pie filling
1 T. lemon juice

Beat cream cheese, sugar, eggs, lemon juice, and vanilla till light and fluffy. Line muffin (cupcake) tins with baking cup liners and place 1 vanilla wafer in each cup. Fill ⅔ full with creamed mixture. Bake at 375° for 15 to 20 minutes. Top each with 1 T. of cherry pie filling; chill.

COMPANY TIME CAKE

- 2 C. flour
- 2 C. sugar
- 2 eggs
- 2 tsp. soda
- 1 C. chopped nuts
- 1 (20 oz.) can crushed pineapple (undrained)
- 1 stick margarine
- 8 oz. cream cheese
- 2 C. powdered sugar
- 1 tsp. vanilla
- 1-2 T. milk

Mix flour, sugar, eggs, soda, nuts and pineapple. Put into greased 9x13-inch pan. Bake at 350° for 40 minutes. Beat margarine with cream cheese. Add powdered sugar, vanilla and milk; beat till smooth. Spread over hot cake. Chill cake at least 24 hours before serving.

FREEBORN FROSTING

2 C. brown sugar
7 T. water
Pinch of salt

2 egg whites
½ tsp. vanilla

Combine all ingredients in top of double boiler, beating with mixer at low speed until mixed. Place over boiling water and beat with mixer at low speed. Cook for 5 minutes. Remove double boiler from heat and continue beating 2 minutes longer. Place double boiler into cold water and continue beating 3 minutes longer. Makes enough for a 9x13-inch cake.

APPLE SPICE CAKE

1 C. sugar
1 egg (beaten)
½ C. oleo
½ C. cold coffee
1 C. chopped peeled raw apples

1 tsp. cinnamon
1 tsp. cloves
Scant tsp. soda
1½ C. sifted flour
Brown sugar & nuts

Cream sugar and oleo; add egg. Add remaining ingredients, except apples. Stir and add apples. Sprinkle with brown sugar and nuts. Pour Into 11x7½-inch pan. Bake at 375° for 40 minutes.

OLD FASHIONED PEACH CAKE

1 box yellow cake mix	1 stick butter
3 eggs	1 C. sugar
1 can peach pie filling	1 C. flour
½ C. nuts	

Mix together cake mix, eggs, pie filling and nuts. Pour into greased and floured 9x13-inch pan. Mix together butter, sugar and flour with a fork until blended. Sprinkle over cake and bake at 350° for 40 to 45 minutes.

RHUBARB CRUNCH

4 C. diced rhubarb
1 C. miniature marshmallows
1 (3 oz.) pkg. strawberry Jello (dry)
1½ C. sugar
½ C. melted butter
1 (2-layer size) yellow cake mix
1 C. water

Combine rhubarb, marshmallows, gelatin and sugar. Spread in bottom of greased 9x13-inch pan. Combine the melted butter and cake mix. Sprinkle on top of rhubarb mixture. Pour 1 C. water over all. Bake at 350° for 1 hour.

COLD WATER COCOA CAKE

½ C. butter
1/8 tsp. salt
1 C. sugar
1 tsp. vanilla
½ C. cocoa

½ C. cold water
2½ C. sifted flour
1 C. cold water
3 egg whites
¾ C. sugar
1⅓ tsp. soda

Cream butter, salt, sugar and vanilla. Blend cocoa and the ½ C. cold water, then add to the creamed ingredients. Blend well. Add the sifted flour and the 1 C. cold water alternately to the creamed mixture. Beat the egg whites until stiff, and add the ¾ C. sugar, and continue to beat to form a stiff meringue. Fold meringue into the batter. Dissolve the soda in a small amount of boiling water and fold into the batter, mixing well. Pour into a greased and floured 9x13-inch pan. Bake at 350° for about 35 minutes.

RHUBARB COBBLER

- 1 C. sugar
- 1 C. flour
- 2 tsp. baking powder
- 1 egg (beaten in cup with milk to fill cup ¾ full)
- Pinch salt
- 2 T. soft shortening
- 1 tsp. vanilla
- 3 C. rhubarb
- 1 C. sugar dissolved in 1 C. hot water

Mix all but last 3 ingredients. Pour into 9x9-inch pan. Spread rhubarb over all. Bake 35 minutes at 375°. Serve with ice cream or whipped topping.

LUSCIOUS LUTHERAN CAKE

1 yellow cakemix (without pudding)
1 (3 oz.) pkg. instant vanilla pudding
1 (8 oz.) carton sour cream
½ C. salad oil
1 C. water

3 eggs
1 (6 oz.) pkg. milk chocolate
chips
½ C. chopped pecans
1 (4 oz.) bar German chocolate

FROSTING:

1 stick soft margarine
8 oz. cream cheese
1 box powdered sugar

1 tsp. vanilla
½ C. chopped pecans (optional)

Mix together first 6 ingredients. Fold in chocolate chips and nuts. Shave all but 4 squares German chocolate into batter. Bake at 350° in greased and floured 9x13-inch pan for 30-40 minutes. Mix frosting ingredients and spread on cooled cake. Shave remaining 4 squares chocolate on top and sprinkle with nuts if desired.

PIE

MINNESOTA PIE

Butterscotch Chiffon Pie............96
Lake of the Woods Choc.Pie 97
Minnesota Rhubarb Pie 98
Pumpkin Pie...............................102
Red Lake Pie Crust....................101
Rhubarb Pie 100
Strawberry Pie...........................99
Swedish Apple Pie 95

SWEDISH APPLE PIE

Apples
1 T. sugar
1 tsp. cinnamon
¾ C. melted butter
1 C. sugar
1 C. flour
1 egg
Pinch of salt
¼ C. nuts (optional)

For 9x9-inch pan, fill ⅔ full of apples. Sprinkle sugar and cinnamon on top. Combine remaining ingredients in bowl and pour over apples. Bake at 350° for 45 minutes.
Note: Peaches or most any fruit can be substituted for apples.

BUTTERSCOTCH CHIFFON PIE

1 envelope unflavored gelatin	2 T. butter
¼ C. cold water	¼ tsp. salt
3 eggs (separated)	½ tsp. vanilla
1 C. brown sugar (packed)	½ tsp. burnt sugar flavoring
1 C. milk (scalded)	¼ C. white sugar
	Baked pie shell

Beat egg yolks until thick and lemon colored. Gradually beat in the brown sugar, then the scalded milk. Add butter and salt and cook over hot water until mixture coats the spoon. Stir in gelatin that has been soaked in the cold water. Cool and add flavorings. After mixture has cooled, beat egg whites until quite stiff, adding the ¼ C. sugar. Fold into the cooled custard mixture. Pour into baked pie shell and chill until firm.

LAKE OF THE WOODS CHOCOLATE PIE

1 (8-inch) baked pie shell
½ C. butter or margarine
¾ C. sugar
1 (1 oz.) sq. chocolate
1 tsp. vanilla
2 eggs
Whipping cream or Cool Whip
Walnuts

Cream butter and add gradually the sugar, creaming well. Blend in chocolate (melted) and cooled, then vanilla. Add eggs, 1 at a time, beating 5 minutes after each addition (with electric mixer use medium speed). Turn into cooled shell. Chill for 1 to 2 hours. Can top with whipping cream or Cool Whip and walnuts. This is Wayne's favorite pie.

MINNESOTA RHUBARB PIE

2 C. hot rhubarb, cooked with small
   amount of water
¾ C. sugar
1 pkg. strawberry Jello

1 large can Carnation milk (whipped)
1 tsp. vanilla
1 prebaked pie shell
Cool Whip

Chill milk, beaters and bowl. To the hot rhubarb add the Jello and cool. Whip the cooled condensed milk and add vanilla. Add to the cooled rhubarb mixture and put into pie shell. Refrigerate and serve with Cool Whip.

STRAWBERRY PIE

1 C. sugar
1 C. water

3 T. Karo white corn syrup
3 T. cornstarch

Bring to a boil. Cook until thick. Add 3 T. strawberry Jello. Let cool. Pour over strawberry lined baked pastry shell. Chill. Serve with whipped topping. (NOTE: May change fruit to fresh peaches and use peach Jello.)

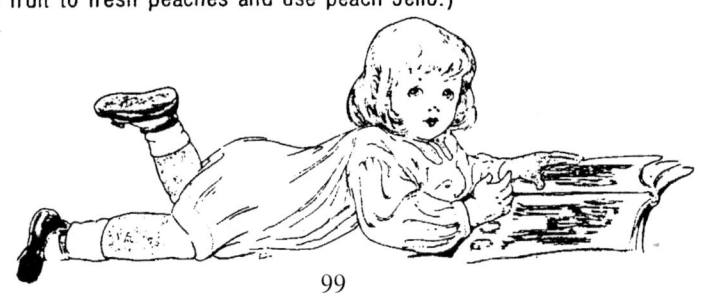

RHUBARB PIE

2 C. cut rhubarb
1½ C. sugar
1 egg

2 T. flour (rounded)
Cream
Cinnamon
Butter

Combine beaten egg, flour and sugar. Add cream to make a paste, pour over rhubarb in unbaked pie crust. Dot with butter and cinnamon. If larger pie is desired increase ingredients proportionately.

RED LAKE PIE CRUST

2½ C. flour
1 tsp. salt
1 C. Crisco
½ C. water
Fruit filling

Measure flour and salt into mixing bowl. Add Crisco and work together until coarse and crumbly. Sprinkle water in a little at a time. Mix with hands to form a ball. Divide in half and place on floured board and roll thin with a rolling pin. Line pie plate. Add filling and roll next crust and cover top. Cut slits in top crust. Bake at 425° for 15 minutes. Lower heat to 375° for another 40-45 minutes or until golden brown.

PUMPKIN PIE (Special Diet)

1 (16 oz.) can pumpkin
1½ tsp. pumpkin pie spice
1 tsp. salt
1 large can evaporated skim milk

¼ C. brown SugarTwin or
  3 tsp. liquid sweetener
2 egg whites

Blend pumpkin and spices then add rest of ingredients and mix well. Put in pie shell. Will make 2 small pies or one large deep dish pie. Bake at 375° for 45-50 minutes or until knife inserted comes out clean.

MAIN DISHES

MINNESOTA MAIN DISHES

Apple Glazed Roast 107
Beans/Macaroni Cass 122
Beef/Broccoli Stir Fry.........123
Beef Turnover.....................133
Cashew Chicken 114
Cheese Meat Loaf...............119
Chicken Biscuits Cass. 121
Chicken Casserole 124
Chippewa 129
Company Chicken...............106
Country Style Ribs 128
Creamed Chicken...............113
Crunchy Chicken 'n Rice 131
Escalloped Chicken 126
Fatless Fried Chicken.........111

Ground Beef Salami 130
Ham Balls 116
Mandarin Chicken Rolls 109
Miss.River Boat Chicken. ...108
Pizza Casserole 120
Quick Sweet & Sour Pork ...125
Special Lasagne 105
Stuffed Green Peppers........112
Supper on a Slice 127
Swedish Fish Bake.............117
Swedish Ham Balls 115
Taco Pie 118
Twin Cities Stroganoff 132
Zucchini Cass.Hot Dish......110

SPECIAL LASAGNE

1 lb. ground beef
1 lb. ground pork
1 pkg. lasagne noodles
1 pkg. frozen chopped spinach
½ pt. cottage cheese
1 C. grated mozzarella cheese
1 can tomato paste
Italian seasoning
3 eggs

Brown meats, drain and add tomato paste and seasoning; set aside. Combine spinach (cooked), cottage cheese and beaten eggs; set aside. Cook noodles and drain. In pan layer meat, noodles, spinach, cheese and end with meat and cheese. Bake at 350° for 45 minutes. Spoon spaghetti-tomato sauce over squares. Makes 8 to 10 servings.

COMPANY CHICKEN

1 chicken
1 C. rice
1 can mushroom soup

1 pkg. dry onion soup mix
1½ soup cans water
Salt

Cut up chicken. Put 1 C. uncooked rice in bottom of roaster. Place chicken pieces over rice. Sprinkle lightly with salt. Mix can of mushroom soup, package dry onion soup mix and 1½ soup cans water. Pour over chicken and rice. Bake at 300° for 3 hours.

APPLE GLAZED ROAST

1 (4-6 lb.) pork shoulder blade Boston roast
1 (14 oz.) jar apple butter
⅓ C. beer

3 T. brown sugar
¼ tsp. ground cinnamon
1/8 tsp. ground cloves

Place meat on rack in shallow pan. Roast in 325° oven for 2 hours. Meanwhile, in a bowl, stir together the apple butter, beer, brown sugar, cinnamon and cloves. Spread apple butter mixture over top and sides of roast. Continue roasting for 1-2 hours more or until meat thermometer registers 170°. Heat any remaining apple butter mixture and pass with meat. Transfer roast to warm serving platter. Makes 10-12 servings.

MISSISSIPPI RIVER BOAT CHICKEN

6 chicken breasts (halves)
12 strips bacon
½ lb. chipped beef

1 (10 oz.) can cream of mushroom
  soup
1 C. sour cream
Sliced almonds

Wrap each breast with bacon strips diagonally. Cover bottom of 9x12-inch pan with chipped beef. Place chicken on the beef. Cover with a mixture of soup and sour cream. Sprinkle top with almonds. Do not salt as the chipped beef seasons it. Bake at 250° for 3½ hours. Cover the last hour. If it starts getting dry add a bit more sour cream. Serves 12.

MANDARIN CHICKEN ROLLS

4 small boneless chicken breasts
1½ tsp. sesame oil
½ tsp. salt
1/8 tsp. pepper
12-16 whole green beans
4 green onions
8 slivers carrots
8 slivers celery
1 C. rice
1 C. orange juice
1 T. cornstarch
1 can mandarin oranges
½ tsp. lemon juice
Cherry tomatoes (optional)

Heat oven to 425°. Spray 2-qt. baking dish. Brush on side of each breast with sesame oil. Sprinkle with salt and pepper. Pound breasts thin and place vegetables in it and roll up. Bake 20-25 minutes. Cook rice and cover until ready to serve. Combine orange juice and cornstarch and bring to a boil. Cook 2-3 minutes. Stir in oranges and lemon juice and heat. Place chicken and rice on large platter. Pour orange sauce over all. Garnish with cherry tomatoes.

ZUCCHINI CASSEROLE HOT DISH

1½ C. water
1½ tsp. salt
1 T. oil
1 tsp. pepper
1 green pepper
1 pt. tomatoes or soup or sauce
½ tsp. paprika

3 C. zucchini (diced)
1 onion (minced)
2 T. uncooked rice
1 lb. ground beef
1 C. diced cheese (cheddar or
    sharp
2 C. toasted bread crumbs

Cook squash in water with ½ tsp. salt. Brown onions, green pepper in oil, then drain. Brown meat, place in casserole with all remaining ingredients and rest of salt. Sprinkle 2 C. toasted bread crumbs on top. Bake 1 hour at 350°. Serve hot.

FATLESS FRIED CHICKEN

4 deboned split chicken breasts (skinned)

1 tsp. seasoned salt
½ tsp. pepper

Sprinkle salt and pepper on both sides of chicken. Place in non-stick surface frying pan and cover. Cook on medium heat for 10 to 15 minutes. Turn chicken and continue cooking on medium heat for about 10 minutes. Remove lid and allow moisture to evaporate and chicken to brown. Makes 4 servings.

STUFFED GREEN PEPPERS

8-10 green peppers
½ C. rice
2 lbs. ground beef
1 C. uncooked oatmeal
1 tsp. salt
¼ tsp. pepper
1 chopped onion

2 beaten eggs
1 T. salad mustard
8 T. catsup
1 C. thick tomato sauce
½ C. water
1 tsp. steak sauce or Worcestershire
    (can use seasoned tomato juice)

Drop green peppers into pan of boiling water. Simmer for 5 to 10 minutes until slightly tender; drain. Cook rice in 2 C. water until tender. Drain and run cold water through to separate. Combine all ingredients, including cooked rice; mix thoroughly. Stuff peppers. Make a sauce of tomato sauce, mixed with water and steak sauce. Pour some sauce over peppers that are placed upright in pan. Baste peppers with sauce several times during baking. Bake at 350° for 1 hour. To prevent burning, place a flat pan of water on rack before the pan of peppers.

CREAMED CHICKEN

3 T. butter
3 T. flour
1½ C. milk
½ C. hot chicken stock or broth

4 C. diced cooked chicken
Pinch of salt
Dash of celery salt
Dash of paprika

Melt butter, stir in flour and seasonings. Slowly pour on milk and stock, stirring constantly. Bring to boiling point, add chicken. You can add ½ C. diced pimento and ½ C. diced mushrooms. Recipe can easily be doubled.

CASHEW CHICKEN

2 chicken bouillon cubes
1¾ C. boiling water
2 T. soy sauce
5 tsp. cornstarch
¼ tsp. ground ginger
3 cooked chicken breasts (diced)

2 T. vegetable oil
2 C. sliced fresh mushrooms
½ C. sliced green onions
1 small green pepper (sliced)
1 (8 oz.) can water chestnuts
Cashews

Combine all but cashews and simmer for 5 to 8 minutes, then mix in cashews and serve on hot cooked rice.

SWEDISH HAM BALLS

1 lb. ground smoked ham
1½ lb. ground lean pork
2 C. bread crumbs
½ C. water
2 eggs (well-beaten)

1 C. milk
½ C. vinegar
1½ C. brown sugar
1 tsp. dry mustard

Combine brown sugar, vinegar, water and mustard. Stir until sugar is dissolved. Combine meats, crumbs, eggs and milk; mix thoroughly. Form in small balls - about the size of golf balls. Place in large casserole or pan. Pour brown sugar mixture over meatballs. Bake in slow 275° oven for 1¼ hours. Baste frequently with brown sugar mixture.

HAM BALLS

1 ¼ lbs. ground smoked ham
1 lb. ground lean pork
½ lb. ground beef

2 eggs
1 ½ C. crushed graham crackers
1 C. milk

SAUCE:
1 can tomato soup
¼ C. vinegar

1 C. brown sugar
1 tsp. dry mustard

Mix ingredients well and form into small balls. Mix the sauce ingredients and pour over meatballs. Put foil on brownie pan and bake at 350° for 1 hour or 1 ½ hours.

SWEDISH FISH BAKE

1 lb. white fish fillets	2 tsp. prepared horseradish
1 can cream of celery soup	2 T. chopped pimiento
1 C. cooked cut green beans	½ tsp. dried dill (crushed)

In ½ pint shallow baking dish, arrange fish in single layer. Bake at 350° for 15 minutes. Spoon off excess liquid. Combine remaining ingredients and pour over fish. Bake 10 minutes more or until done. Stir sauce before serving. Makes 3 servings.

TACO PIE

1 lb. ground beef
½ C. chopped onion
2 env. taco seasoning mix
¾ C. Bisquick
1¼ C. milk

3 eggs
1 C. shredded cheddar cheese
¼ head of lettuce
1 tomato (diced)
⅓ C. sliced ripe olives

Grease square 8x8x2-inch baking dish. Cook and stir ground beef and onion; drain. Stir in seasoning mix and spoon into pan. Beat Bisquick, milk and eggs with wire whisk or hand beater until smooth, about 1 minute. Pour into pan and bake at 400° for about 25 minues or until knife inserted in center comes out clean. Sprinkle with cheese and bake until cheese is melted, about 2 minutes. Cool for 5 minutes. Garnish with lettuce, tomato, olives and sour cream, if desired.

CHEESE MEAT LOAVES

2 lbs. hamburger
2¾ C. fresh bread cubes (5 slices)
¾ C. diced onion
2 T. parsley
1 tsp. salt
¼ tsp. basil (optional)
¼ tsp. pepper
1 C. veg. soup or chicken gumbo
¼ C. milk
8 fingers of cheese

Mix all ingredients well, except for cheese. Shape into 8 meat loaves, putting a stick of cheese in center of loaf. Place in greased baking pan and bake at 300° for 1½ hours or 35 minutes in microwave. Put sauce on the last 10 minutes.

For Sauce: Mix ¾ C. catsup, ¼ C. mustard and ¾ C. brown sugar.

PIZZA CASSEROLE

1½ lbs. ground beef
1 C. chopped onion
1 C. chopped green pepper
1/8 tsp. garlic powder
½ tsp. oregano
Salt

½ C. water
1/8 tsp. hot salt
1 (15 oz.) can tomato sauce
1 env. spaghetti sauce mix
Mozzarella cheese

TOPPING:
1 C. milk
1 T. oil

2 eggs
1 C. flour

Brown beef and drain, stir in rest of ingredients, except cheese and simmer for 10 minutes. Pour into 13x9-inch pan and cover with sliced mozzarella cheese. Beat batter for 2 minutes. Pour on batter to cover completely and sprinkle with parmesan. Bake at 400° for 25 to 30 minutes.

CHICKEN BISCUITS CASSEROLE

- 1 can cond. cream of chicken soup
- ¾ C. milk
- 2 C. chopped cooked chicken
- 1 pkg. frozen vegetables (broccoli, cauliflower & carrot mixture)
- 1 C. shredded cheddar cheese
- 1 can French fried onions
- 1 C. biscuit mix
- ⅓ C. milk

Thaw and drain vegetables. Combine soup, milk, chicken, vegetables, ½ C. cheese and ½ can onions. Spread mixture into a greased 8x12-inch baking dish. Bake, uncovered at 425° for 10 minutes. Meanwhile, combine biscuit mix and milk to form a soft dough. Drop by spoonfuls to make biscuits. Bake, uncovered at 425° for 20 to 25 minutes or until biscuits are golden. Top biscuits with remaining cheese and onions; bake for 3 to 5 more minutes.

BEANS AND MACARONI CASSEROLE

1 lb. dried beans (any kind)	3 carrots
1 lb. macaroni (any shape)	Zucchini
1 bay leaf	Other fresh vegetables as available
6 cloves garlic	1 C. grated parmesan cheese
3 fresh tomatoes	Oil
3 stalks celery	

Soak beans overnight with bay leaf. Cook beans and bay leaf until tender. Reserve cooking liquid. Cook macaroni and drain. Saute garlic and fresh vegetables in oil. Mix cooked beans, macaroni, sauted vegetables in a baking dish. Add enough of the cooking liquid from the beans to keep casserole moist. Top with 1 C. grated parmesan cheese. Bake, uncovered in 300° oven until it bubbles and the cheese starts to brown. Serves 10.

BEEF AND BROCCOLI STIR FRY

⅓ C. water
2 T. soy sauce
2 T. dry sherry
1 tsp. ground ginger
1½ tsp. cornstarch

1 small garlic clove (crushed)
¼ tsp. red pepper flakes
1½ lb. round steak (stripped)
1 T. vegetable oil
4 C. broccoli

Combine first 7 ingredients in shallow dish. Add beef, cover and refrigerate for 30 minutes. Remove, drain and reserve marinade. Heat oil in skillet. Add beef and stir-fry for about 4 minutes. Add broccoli and stir-fry for about 3 minutes. Pour marinade over mixture. Cook and stir until thickened, about 1 minute longer.

CHICKEN CASSEROLE

1 pkg. noodles
  (8 or 10 oz., cooked as directed)
2-3 C. chicken or family size tuna
1 C. cheddar cheese (grated)
1 small pkg. slivered almonds
  (browned in butter)

1 green pepper (chopped)
1 can asparagus (use liquid)
1 C. Miracle Whip
1 can cream of mushroom soup
1 can cream of chicken soup
Top with corn flake crumbs

Bake at 350° for 1 hour. Top with corn flake crumbs.

QUICK SWEET AND SOUR PORK

- 1 carrot (sliced thin)
- 2 T. cooking oil
- 1 lb. boneless pork, cut into 1'' cubes
- 1 (15¼ oz.) can pineapple chunks
- ½ C. corn syrup (dark or light) or honey
- ¼ C. vinegar
- 2 T. catsup
- 2 T. soy sauce
- 1 clove of garlic (minced)
- 2 T. cornstarch
- ½ C. green pepper pieces (sliced)
- ½ C. onion pieces (sliced)

Heat and brown the first 3 ingredients. Mix next 6 ingredients and bring to a boil and simmer until done. Mix cornstarch and 2 T. water. Add to pork with pepper and onion. Boil for 2 minutes, stirring constantly. Serve over rice. Serves 4.

ESCALLOPED CHICKEN

1 pt. cooked chicken (cut in cubes)
1 pt. chicken broth
2 T. flour
2 T. shortening
3 C. bread crumbs
⅓ C. melted butter

1 tsp. sage
¼ tsp. salt
1 T. chopped onion
Chopped green pepper
Chopped celery

Mix all together and bake at 350° for 30 minutes.

SUPPER ON A SLICE

- 1½ lbs. ground beef
- 1 small can evaporated milk
- ½ C. bread crumbs
- 1 egg
- 1 medium onion (grated)
- 1 tsp. prepared mustard
- ½ tsp. salt
- ½ tsp. garlic salt
- ½ tsp. thyme
- 1 tsp. Accent
- 1/8 tsp. pepper
- 2 tsp. Worcestershire sauce
- 1 C. grated cheddar cheese
- 1 loaf French bread (halved lengthwise)

Combine the first 13 ingredients. Place bread, crust side down on a sheet of foil, leaving 3-inch edge, spread beef mixture evenly over bread. Bring foil up around each bread half, crimping ends to form boat-shaped holders. Bake at 350° for 30 minutes. Sprinkle some cheese on top and bake for 5 minutes longer. I use cheddar and monterey cheese on top. Cut bread diagonally to serve.

COUNTRY STYLE RIBS

4 lbs. country style ribs
¼ C. cooking oil
1 C. chopped onion
1 clove garlic (minced)
1 (8 oz.) can tomato sauce
¼ C. water
¼ C. brown sugar

¼ C. lemon juice
2 T. mustard
2 T. Worcestershire sauce
1 tsp. salt
1 tsp. celery seed
¼ tsp. pepper

In Dutch oven cook ribs, covered in boiling salted water for 45 to 60 minutes or until ribs are tender; drain. In saucepan cook onion and garlic in oil until tender but not brown. Stir in remaining ingredients, simmer uncovered for 15 minutes. Brush with sauce until ribs are coated well. Makes 6 servings. To prepare the oven, place hot ribs in shallow roasting pan. Pour sauce over ribs and bake at 350° for 25 minutes. Baste occasionally with sauce.

CHIPPEWA

- 1 (10¾ oz.) can cond. cream of chicken soup
- ¾ C. milk
- ¼ tsp. seasoned salt
- 2 C. (10 oz.) chopped cooked chicken
- 1 (1 lb.) pkg. frozen broccoli, carrots & carrots (thawed & well drained)
- 1 C. (4 oz.) shredded cheddar cheese
- 1 can (2.8 oz.) French fried onions
- 1 C. biscuit mix
- 1 egg (slightly beaten)
- ¼ C. milk

Combine soup, milk, salt, chicken, vegetables, ½ C. cheese and ½ can French fried onions. Spread mixture into a greased 8x12-inch baking dish. Bake, uncovered at 425° for 10 minutes. Meanwhile combine biscuit mix, egg and milk to form a soft dough. Spoon over hot chicken mixture to form a lattice deisgn. Bake, uncovered at 425° for 20 to 25 minutes or until biscuits are golden. Top lattice with remaining cheese and onions; bake for 3 to 5 minutes or until cheese melts and onions are lightly browned.

GROUND BEEF SALAMI

4 lbs. ground beef (80% lean)
1 tsp. garlic powder
¼ tsp. mustard seed
6 T. Morton tender quick salt

2 C. water
½ tsp. onion powder
2 T. liquid smoke

Blend all together and form into 3-4 logs; wrap in foil. Refrigerate for 24 hours. Poke holes in bottom of foil and place on broiler pan with water underneath. Bake at 325° for 90 minutes.

CRUNCHY CHICKEN'N RICE BAKE

1 can cream of mushroom soup
2 C. milk
2 (5 oz. ea.) cans chicken
1 C. rice (uncooked)
1 can cut green beans (drained)
1 small can mushrooms
2 T. chopped pimento
1 C. grated cheddar cheese
1 (3 oz.) can French fried onions

Combine ingredients. Save out ½ of cheese and onions. Pour into greased 2-quart casserole. Bake, covered at 350° for 40 minutes. Top with remaining cheese and onions. Bake, uncovered for 5 minutes longer

TWIN CITIES STROGANOFF

⅔ can fried onion rings
  or 1 T. Lipton's dry onion soup
Fresh or canned mushrooms (optonal)
1 can mushroom soup
½ C. sour cream

1-2 T. poppy seeds
1 egg
Hungry Jack mix
1 lb. ground chuck
  (browned & drained)

Mix first 5 ingredients and pour over hamburger in casserole. From a box of Hungry Jack biscuits arrange a ring of biscuits around the inside edge of casserole. Beat 1 egg, ½ C. sour cream and 1-2 T. poppy seeds. Pour over biscuits and bake at 350° for 30 minutes. Remove from oven and add ⅓ can onion rings to center of casserole. Return to oven to brown.

BEEF TURNOVER

1 env. (1¼ oz.) beef flavor
  mushroom mix (Lipton dry soup)
1 lb. ground beef
¼ C. chopped onion
1 C. shredded cheddar cheese
3 pkgs. crescent rolls

Brown ground beef and onion; add mushroom mix. Add cheese and place large spoon meat on crescent roll. Seal and place on ungreased cookie sheet. Bake at 350° for 15 minutes.

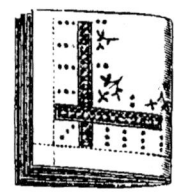

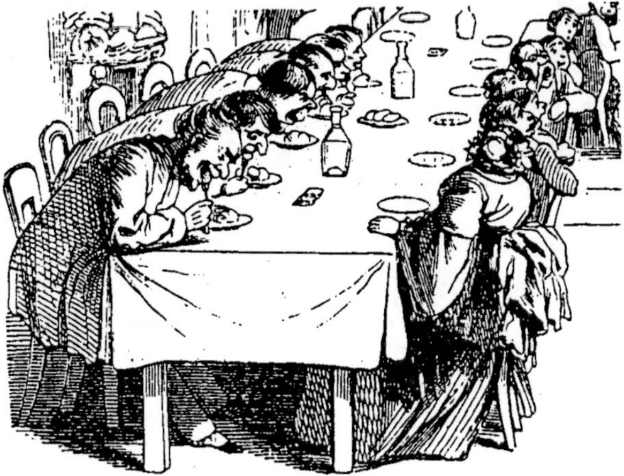

BREAD

MINNESOTA BREAD

Banana Bread..............................143
Breakfast Coffee Cake...............138
Dinner Rolls...............................140
Gingerbread...............................144
Grapenut Bread.........................141
Mom's Ice Box Rolls...................142
Nut Bread..................................137
Nutty Pork & Bean Bread..........139
Pecan Apple Bread.....................145
Pumpkin Swirl Bread................146

NUT BREAD

3 C. flour
1 C. sugar
1 tsp. salt
4 tsp. baking powder

2 eggs
1 C. milk
¾ C. chopped nuts

Beat eggs well. Add sugar and milk. Sift flour, salt and baking powder together. Add to egg mixture. Add nuts. Pour into greased loaf pan and let stand for 20 minutes. Bake in moderate oven at 350° for 1 hour.

BREAKFAST COFFEE CAKE

½ C. butter or oleo	1 tsp. baking soda
¾ C. white sugar	½ tsp. salt
½ C. brown sugar	1 tsp. cinnamon
2 eggs	1 tsp. nutmeg
2 C. flour	1 C. nuts (chopped)
1 tsp. baking powder	1 C. buttermilk

TOPPING:

½ C. brown sugar	1 tsp. cinnamon

Cream first 4 ingredients. Sift dry ingredients together and add to the creamed mixture with the buttermilk. Pour into greased 9x13-inch pan. Sprinkle topping over top. Cover and refrigerate overnight. Bake at 350° for 30 minutes.

NUTTY PORK AND BEAN BREAD

- 1 (16 oz.) can pork and beans
- 3 eggs
- 3 C. flour
- 2 C. sugar
- 1 C. raisins
- 1 C. boiling water
- 1 C. vegetable oil
- 1 tsp. soda
- 1 tsp. cinnamon
- ½ tsp. baking powder
- 1 C. nuts

Put beans in blender to puree. Let set. Pour boiling water over raisins. Let set. Beat eggs. Add oil and sugar. Add dry ingredients. Bake 50 minutes in 325° oven or until done in 2 loaf pans.

DINNER ROLLS

POUR 1½ C. warm water into bowl.
ADD 1½-2 pkgs. yeast
Let stand few minutes, stir to dissolve.

ADD:

2 C. flour	⅓ C. soft butter
¼ C. sugar	1 egg
1½ tsp. salt	

Beat on medium mixer until smooth. Add 2½ C. flour. Knead until smooth. Cover, let rise about 30-60 minutes until light. Make into rolls. Rise. Bake at 375° for 20-30 minutes (30 minutes for sandwich rolls).

GRAPENUT BREAD

1 C. grapenuts
2 C. buttermilk
2 C. sugar
2 eggs

4 C. sifted flour
2 tsp. baking powder
1 tsp. soda
Salt

Soak grapenuts in buttermilk for 1 hour. Add sugar, eggs, flour, baking powder, soda and salt. Pour into 2 greased bread pans and bake at 350° For 45 minutes or until golden brown. (Low Fat Recipe.)

MOM'S ICE BOX ROLLS

1 T. yeast
½ C. warm water
1 C. hot water
¾ C. shortening
½ tsp. salt

½ C. sugar
7-8 C. flour
1 C. mashed potatoes (2 medium)
2 eggs

Soften yeast in warm water. Pour hot water over shortening, salt and one half of the sugar. Add yeast and 1½ C. flour, mashed potatoes and eggs. Beat and let rise for 2 hours. Add remaining sugar and flour; knead. Let rise again until double. Form rolls, let rise and bake at 425° for 12 minutes. Note: After all flour is added, the dough may be refrigerated overnight, made into rolls and baked in the morning.

BANANA BREAD

- ½ C. butter or margarine
- 1 C. sugar
- 2 eggs
- 1½ C. mashed bananas
- 1 tsp. lemon juice
- 2 C. sifted all-purpose flour
- 1½ tsp. baking powder
- ¾ tsp. soda
- ½ tsp. salt
- ¼ C. dairy sour cream
- ½ C. chopped walnuts

Cream together butter and sugar. Add eggs, one at a time, beating well. Combine bananas and lemon juice; add to sugar mixture and beat well. Add dry ingredients alternately with sour cream. Fold in nuts and pour into two 9x5x3-inch loaf pans. Bake at 375° for 35 to 45 minutes. Makes 2 loaves.

GINGERBREAD

1 C. sour milk
2 ½ C. flour
¼ C. shortening
1 egg
1 C. molasses (sorghum)
½ C. sugar

1 tsp. soda
½ tsp. baking powder
½ tsp. salt
1 tsp. cinnamon
1 tsp. ginger

Mix and bake at 375°.

PECAN APPLE BREAD

½ C. oleo (softened)
1 C. sugar
2 eggs
2 T. milk
1 tsp. vanilla
¼ tsp. butter flavoring
¼ tsp. lemon flavoring
2 C. flour
1 tsp. baking powder
1 tsp. soda
1 C. chopped apples
½ C. pecans

Cream ½ C. oleo and sugar together; add rest of ingredients. Bake at 350° for about 1 hour. (1 loaf)

PUMPKIN SWIRL BREAD

1 (8 oz.) pkg. cream cheese (softened)
¼ C. sugar
1 egg
1 ¾ C. flour
1 ½ C. sugar
1 tsp. soda
1 tsp. cinnamon
½ tsp. salt
¼ tsp. nutmeg
1 C. canned pumpkin
½ C. margarine
1 egg
1 ⅓ C. water

Combine cream cheese, sugar and egg; set aside. Combine flour, sugar, soda, cinnamon, salt and nutmeg. Mix pumpkin, oleo, egg and water; add to dry ingredients, mixing just until moistened. Reserve 2 C. batter and pour rest into greased 9x5-inch loaf pan. Pour cream mixture over batter. Top with rest of batter and cut thru with knife to make a swirl effect. Bake at 350° for 1 hour and 10 minutes. Cool for 5 minutes, then remove from pan.

CANDY

MINNESOTA CANDY

Chocolate Fudge 152
Divinity...153
Peanut Clusters 149
Peanut Butter Balls......................150
Sweet Minnesota Girl Fudge.........151

PEANUT CLUSTERS

6 sq. almond bark (¾-1 lb.)
1 (12 oz.) pkg. chocolate chips
1 pkg. Spanish peanuts

Melt almond bark over low heat or in double boiler. Add chocolate chips and stir until melted. Add Spanish peanuts and mix. Drop on waxed paper. Refrigerate or keep in a cool dry place.

PEANUT BUTTER BALLS

2½ C. powdered sugar
1 stick butter
3 C. Rice Krispies

2 C. peanut butter
1 tsp. vanilla

Mix all ingredients together and roll into balls. Refrigerate on sheet pan for 1 hour or overnight. Dip balls in melted chocolate almond bark. Put dipped balls back in refrigerator for awhile before storing.

SWEET MINNESOTA GAL FUDGE

2 C. sugar
3 T. margarine
½ tsp. salt
½ C. miniature marshmallows

1½ C. chocolate chips
1 tsp. vanilla
1 C. evaporated milk
⅔ C. chopped nuts

Combine sugar, oleo, salt and milk in a large electric skillet. Set thermostat at 280°. Bring to a boil and boil for 5 minutes, stirring constantly. Turn off skillet and add the rest of the ingredients and stir until marshmallows and chocolate chips are melted and smooth. Put in 8x8-inch pan and cool. Makes 2 lbs.

CHOCOLATE FUDGE

1 cube butter or margarine
2 sq. unsweetened chocolate (if cocoa
   is used more margarine is needed)
1 box powdered sugar

1 slightly beaten egg
1 tsp. vanilla
1 C. nuts

Put box of powdered sugar in a bowl. Melt in saucepan the margarine and chocolate squares. Pour over sugar. Add egg, vanilla and nuts. Mix well and spread in 8-inch buttered pan. Refrigerate at all times.

MICROWAVE

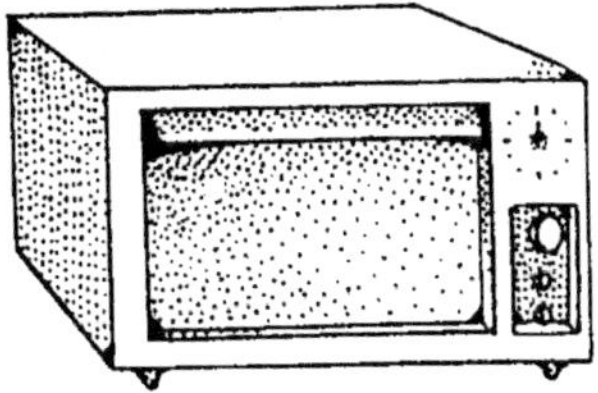

MINNESOTA MICROWAVE COOKING

Microwave Stuffed Mushrooms ...158
Scalloped Corn...........................157

SCALLOPED CORN *(Microwave)*

1 can reg. corn
1 can cream-style corn
1 small tub sour cream
1 Jiffy corn mix
1 egg
1 stick butter

Mix together and cook on High for 10 minutes. Turn ¼ turn and cook for 10 minutes. Turn ¼ turn and cook for 3 to 5 minutes.

MICROWAVE STUFFED MUSHROOMS

24 medium mushrooms
4 green onions
1 medium red pepper (diced)
1 (6½ oz.) can crab meat (drained)

½ C. blanched almonds (chopped)
½ C. mayonnaise
2 T. cooking or dry sherry
½ tsp. salt

Remove and chop stems. In 2-quart casserole, place stems, chopped green onions and red pepper. Cover with lid and cook on High for 2½ to 3 minutes until tender. Stir in the crab meat and remaining ingredients. Fill the caps with mixture. Line a large platter with paper towels. Arrange the caps in a circle. Cook for 5 to 6 minutes till hot. Makes 24 at 65 calories each.

Here's a list of some of the best cookbooks in the western half of the Universe. Just check 'em off, stick a check in an envelope with this page, and we'll get your books off to you pronto. Oh, yes, add $2.00 for shipping and handling for the first book and then fifty cents more for each additional one. If you order over $30.00, forget the shipping and handling.

Mini Cookbooks
(Only 3 1/2 x 5) With Maxi Good Eatin' - 160 pages - $5.95

- □ Arizona Cooking
- □ Dakota Cooking
- □ Illinois Cooking
- □ Indiana Cooking
- □ Iowa Cookin'
- □ Kansas Cookin'
- □ Kentucky Cookin'
- □ Michigan Cooking
- □ Minnesota Cookin'
- □ Missouri Cookin'
- □ New Jersey Cooking
- □ New Mexico Cooking
- □ New York Cooking
- □ Ohio Cooking
- □ Pennsylvania Cooking
- □ Wisconsin Cooking
- □ Amish Mennonite Apple Cookbook
- □ Amish Mennonite Pumpkin Cookbook
- □ Amish & Mennonite
- □ Strawberry Cookbook
- □ Apples! Apples! Apples!
- □ Apples Galore
- □ Berries! Berries! Berries!
- □ Berries Galore!
- □ Bountiful Blueberries

- □ Cherries! Cherries! Cherries!
- □ Citrus! Citrus! Citrus!
- □ Cooking With Cider
- □ Cooking With Spirits
- □ Cooking with Fresh Herbs
- □ Cooking with Garlic
- □ Cooking With Things Go Baa
- □ Cooking With Things Go Cluck
- □ Cooking With Things Go Moo
- □ Cooking With Things Go Oink
- □ Cooking With Things Go Splash
- □ Crockpot Cookbook
- □ Good Cookin' From the
- □ Hill People Plain People
- □ Holiday & Get-together Cookbook
- □ How to Make Salsa
- □ Kid Cookin'
- □ Kid Fun
- □ Kid Money
- □ Kid Pumpkin Fun Book
- □ Midwest Small Town Cookin'
- □ Muffins Cookbook
- □ Nuts! Nuts! Nuts!
- □ Off To College Cookbook

In-Between Cookbooks
(5 1/2 x 8 1/2) - 150 pages - $9.95

- □ Amish Ladies Cookbook - Old Husbands
- □ Amish Ladies Cookbook - Young Husbands
- □ The Adaptable Apple Cookbook
- □ Bird Up! Pheasant Cookbook
- □ Breads! Breads! Breads!
- □ Camp Cookin'
- □ Civil War Cookin', Stories, 'n Such
- □ Cookin' Ala Nude
- □ Cooking for a Crowd
- □ Country Cooking
- □ Eating Ohio
- □ The Cow Puncher's Cookbook
- □ Recipes from my Amish Heritage
- □ Farmers Market Cookbook
- □ Feast of Moons Indian Cookbook
- □ Fire Fighters Cookbook
- □ Football Mom's
- □ Halloween Fun Book
- □ Herbal Cookery

Story Book $6.95

- □ Veggie Talk Coloring & Story Book
- □ Working Girl Cookbook
- □ Super Simple Cookin'
- □ Squash Cookbook
- □ Some Like It Hot
- □ Peaches! Peaches! Peaches!

- Hunting in the Nude Cookbook
- Ice Cream Cookbook
- Indian Cooking Cookbook
- Little 'Ol Blue-Haired Church-Lady Cookbook
- Mad About Garlic
- Make the Play All-Sport Cookbook
- Motorcycler's Wild Critter Cookbook
- Outdoor Cooking for Outdoor Men
- Shhh Cookbook
- Soccer Mom's Cookbook

- Southwest Ghost Town Cookbook
- Turn of the Century Cooking
- Vegan Vegetarian Cookbook
- Venison Cookbook

Biggie Cookbooks
(5 1/2 x 8 1/2) - 200 plus pages - $11.95
- A Cookbook for them what Ain't Done a Whole lot of Cookin'
- Aphrodisiac Cooking
- Back to the Supper Table Cookbook
- Cooking for One (ok, Maybe two)

- Covered Bridges Cookbook
- Depression Times Cookbook
- Dial-a-Dream Cookbook
- Flat Out, Dirt Cheap Cookin'
- Hormone Helper Cookbook
- Real Men Cook on Sunday Cookbook
- The I-got-Funner-things-to do Cookbook
- Victorian Sunday Dinners

HEARTS 'N TUMMIES COOKBOOK CO.
1854 - 345th Avenue
Wever, Iowa 52658

1-800-571-BOOK

Name _____

Address _____

_____